Chess

Beginners

Learn The Rules, Strategy, Openings,
Queen's Gambit & More

Golden Knights

Ten Benefits Of Playing Chess:

Develops perspective
Improves memory
Increases intelligence
Deepens focus
Elevates creativity
Boosts planning skills
Increases self-awareness
Protects against dementia
Problem-solving skills
Social and relationship-building skills

"Every chess master was once a beginner."

- Irving Chernev

Table Of Contents

Introduction

Chess is a game of strategy that involves two players. Originally, it was a board game, but today it has evolved beyond that so that you can play it virtually, or even against various forms of artificial intelligence. Millions of people around the world play chess every day, some for fun, and some professionally. This book will give you all the information you need to become either of those people.

Chess is a game of skill, and the more effort you put into learning and practicing, the better you'll get overtime. Chess is also a zero-sum game. This means that there'll be a winner and a loser in each match (with the exception of a few games that end in draws). If you lose a lot as a beginner, you shouldn't despair. That's how we all learn.

Playing chess will help you think strategically. As a chess player, you are in a way, like a general commanding an army. Each chess piece is a valuable asset that needs to be properly utilized if you are to win the game.

The strategic nature of chess is rooted in its very origins. Chess, as we know it in the modern-day, was preceded by similar games, all of which mimicked battle formations. As far back as the 6th century, variations of the game have existed in India, China, Mongolia, Japan, and several other Asian countries.

Chess first arrived in the West during the 10th century when it was introduced in Europe. A lot of modern-day terms used in chess have Persian origins. For example, the word "chess" originates from the word "Shah," which means "King." The term Checkmate evolved from the phrase "Shah Mat," which means "the King is helpless."

In Europe, chess grew in popularity over the centuries despite being sanctioned by the church and the aristocracy. However, people from different regions played by different rules. It wasn't until the 19th century that modern international standard chess rules were clearly outlined.

The first international chess championships were held in 1851, and that's when the rules of the game were set in stone. Today, no matter what country you are in, or what language you speak, you will play chess by the same rules. There is even a single global governing body known as FIDE (The

International Chess Federation) that oversees chess competitions.

So, as you join the global community of chess players, this book will be your guide. Firstly, it will teach you all the rules of the game. Secondly, it will teach you the fundamentals of chess strategy, and give you a framework that you can use to develop your skills. Thirdly, it will give you a roadmap that you can use to transform yourself from a beginner to a master. Your journey begins here.

PART 1: THE RULES OF THE GAME

Chapter 1: The Chessboard

The standard chessboard is a square grid that consists of eight rows and eight columns. For technical purposes, the rows are called ranks, and the columns are called files. Each little square on the chessboard is called a tile. In total, there are 64 tiles on the chessboard. There are light-colored and dark-colored tiles, arranged in alternating order throughout the board.

According to standard chess notation, the ranks (rows) of the chessboard are assigned the numbers 1 to 8 from the bottom (the row closest to the first player) to the top. The files (columns) of the chessboard are assigned small letters "a" to "h" from left to right (from the perspective of the first player).

The following diagram shows a chessboard with ranks, files, and tile names:

8	a8	b8	c8	d8	e8	f8	g8	h8
7	a7	b7	c7	d7	e7	f7	g7	h7
6	a6	b6	c6	d6	e6	f6	g6	h6
5	a5	b5	c5	d5	e5	f5	g5	h5
4	a4	b4	c4	d4	e4	f4	g4	h4
3	a3	b3	c3	d3	e3	f3	g3	h3
2	a2	b2	c2	d2	e2	f2	g2	h2
1	a1	b1	c1	d1	e1	f1	g1	h1
	a	b	c	d	e	f	g	h

As you can see in the diagram, each tile on the board is named according to its file and rank coordinates. For example, the tile on the first file and the first rank (the one on the lower-left corner) is named "a1." The tile on the fourth file and the seventh column is named "d7."

Whenever you see "a1," "d7" or any other small letter and number combination come up when you are reading about chess, you'll know that they refer to the specific tiles that you see in the above diagram.

All chess matches start with the same setup. The pieces on the board are divided into light-colored pieces and dark-colored pieces. Again, like with the chessboard, the exact colors of the pieces may change from one chess set to the next, but as a matter of convention, the light-colored pieces are called white, and the dark-colored ones are called black.

Both the white and black pieces come in sets of 16. Each player gets one King, one Queen, two Rooks, two Bishops, two Knights, and eight Pawns.

The following image shows a chessboard set at the initial position:

For the white player, the eight Pawns fill up the second rank. For the black player, the eight Pawns fill-up the seventh rank. As for the other pieces, they are arranged on both the first and eighth ranks in the following order: Rook, Knight, Bishop, Queen, King, Bishop, Knight, and Rook.

Traditionally, the first four files (a, b, c, and d) are collectively referred to as "Queen's side." The remaining four files (e, f, g, and h) are collectively known as "King's side." You should note that the initial positions for the King and Queen from the perspective of the white player are different than they are from the perspective of the black player. That's not a mistake; the board is set up that way by design.

Chapter 2: Chess Notation

Chess notation is a method of recording events in a chess match in order to keep score. If you have ever seen a movie or TV show about chess, you probably recall moments where characters scribble down seemingly cryptic sets of letters and numbers on a chart. For example, in the Queen's Gambit (the Netflix Series), the protagonist, Beth Haarman, is often depicted taking down notes while playing chess matches. That's what chess notation is — a standardized way of describing chess matches play by play so that other people looking at the transcript can know exactly what went on during the match.

It is not necessary to learn chess notation unless you plan on competing in live events, or you want to have a better understanding of the chessboard. It is very possible to learn how to play the game and to get good at it just by knowing the piece movements. Technical knowledge of chess notation is not mandatory.

Even so, it would be beneficial for you to read this section of the book because we will be using chess notation to elaborate on some of the examples that we will be using in subsequent chapters. Chess notation, particularly standard notation, is fairly easy to understand, so don't worry, there isn't any complex math involved here.

In this book, we will try as much as possible to use visual illustrations in the examples we cite, so you should be able to follow and get a general idea of the concepts we are describing even if you aren't yet fully comfortable with chess notation. Some of the images will depict the chessboard at various stages of play with some pieces missing. Chess notation will help you understand how we got to those moves, and it can also help you picture the next moves that can be made in some cases.

With each image in the book, take the time to study the positions of the pieces and to read the notations for the specific moves that we are describing. It will take some time before you can fully get your head around the notations, but I promise you that it will be worthwhile. Learning notation will save you a lot of time in the future and it will expand your ability to understand other chess material too.

There are various systems of notation that have been created in order to record and share information about chess. There are notation systems for humans and other more technical notations that are meant for computer programs. Here, we will look at just two types of notations, both of which are meant for humans.

The first one is algebraic chess notation. It is the default standard international notation that everyone uses today. We will look at it in detail. The second one is descriptive chess notation, which is also known as English notation. This one was widely used in English-speaking countries until the 1970s, so you might still come across it if you study chess texts that were published back then, or if you interact with older chess players. We'll look at it briefly so you can have a basic understanding of how it works.

Algebraic Chess Notation

This notation is very compact and very easy to understand. In the previous chapter, you saw the board with ranks 1 to 8 and files "a" to "h," and coordinate-based names for each tile. That naming system is part of algebraic chess notation.

In algebraic notation, the chess pieces are represented by designated capital letters or figurines. The King is represented by "K", the Queen by "Q", the Rook by "R", the Bishop by "B", the Knight by "N" and the Pawn by "P". Note that each piece is represented by the first letter in its name, except for Knight which is designated the letter "N" to distinguish it from the King.

The following table shows a list of the chess pieces, and their algebraic notations, both in letter form and in figurines:

♟	P A W N	P
♞	K N I G H T	N
♝	B I S H O P	B
♜	R O O K	R
♛	Q U E E N	Q
♚	K I N G	K

When using standard notation, the pieces must be noted in uppercase (capital) to distinguish them from the file names. For example, you must write "B" for Bishop so that you can tell it apart from "b" for the second file.

Recording Games In Standard Notation

There's a clear set of rules that you need to follow when using standard algebraic notation. When a player moves a piece, you need to write, first, the capital letter denoting the piece, followed by the algebraic name of the tile where the piece lands.

For example, a move where the Bishop lands on tile b4 would be written down as Bb4.

The Pawn is the only piece that is exempted from this rule. When notating a movement by a Pawn, you can leave out the uppercase letter P. Therefore when a Pawn moves to e4, you'll record that move as e4. The person reading your notes will immediately know that it's a Pawn movement.

Look at the following image, and try to figure out how the movement indicated by the arrow should be notated:

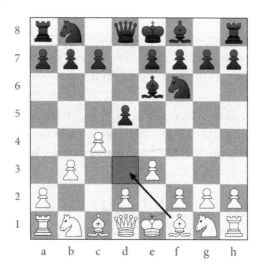

Since the arrow shows that the Bishop will land on d3, the correct notation for that move is Bd3.

Now that you get the general rule, let's look at how you would write down moves that are more complex.

In instances where more than one particular type of piece could have moved to the same tile on the same turn, you need to write the move down in a way that will ensure you identify the specific piece that made the move. To avoid ambiguity, the file and rank of the tile from which the piece moved should be added to the notation. It should be inserted after the capital letter representing the piece, but before the coordinates of the tile where the piece lands.

For example, let's say that two Rooks could have landed on d5. If the two Rooks originate from the same rank, we can write Rbd5 to show that the Rook in questions originated from file b. on the other hand, if the Rooks are from the same file, you can write down R3d5 to clarify the rank from which the Rook originates.

In cases where a piece captures the piece on the tile in which it lands, we use the small (lowercase) letter "x" to indicate the capture. The "x" is added to the notation right before the coordinates of the landing tile are added. For example, Bxf6 means that the Bishop has captured the piece on tile f6.

When a Pawn makes a capture, the file from which that Pawn originates has to be added to the notation before the "x." For example, we write cxd5 when a Pawn from file c captures a piece on d5.

For moves that result in a Check, a plus sign "+" is added at the end to indicate that the other player's King has been put in Check. For example, if the same move as the one before had resulted in a Check, it would have been written down as Bxf6+ .

For moves that result in Checkmate, a hashtag "#" sign is added at the end to notate the Checkmate. Let's look at the following image and figure out how we would record the move indicated by the arrow:

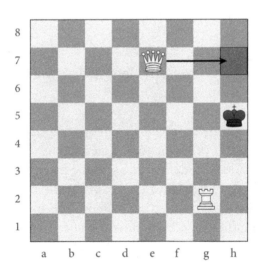

The correct notation for the move in the image is Qh7#.

There are a few other special moves that you'll come to understand as you read on, but we are just going to mention them right now.

The first move is called kingside castling, and it is recorded as 0-0. The second move is called queenside castling, and it's recorded as 0-0-0. This will be further discussed later on.

The third move is called Pawn promotion. It's where a Pawn, upon reaching the opposite side of the chessboard, is promoted to a Queen, Rook, Bishop, or Knight (depending on the player's choice). The notation for this move would include, first, the originating square for the Pawn, then a dash, then the landing square for the Pawn, then an equal sign, then the capital letter representing the piece to which the Pawn has been promoted. For example, if a Pawn moves from f7 to f8, and the player chooses to promote it to a Queen, this move would be written down as f7-f8=Q.

As per the standard rules of the game, the white player goes first. All the moves are listed in pairs until one of the players achieves a Checkmate. If the white player wins, the result is written as 1-0. If the black player wins, it's written as 0-1.

Descriptive Notation

In this notation, all the pieces are represented by the first letter in their names, except for the Knight, which is represented by Kt. So, King is K, Queen is Q, Rook is R, Bishop is B, and the Pawn is P.

The left half of the chessboard (from the white player's perspective) is called the queenside, and the right half is called kingside. The individual tiles have two or three letter names as shown in the following diagram. Additionally, notice that each tile has two names, one from the point of view of the white player, and the other from the point of view of the black player:

QR1 QR8	QN1 QN8	QB1 QB8	Q1 Q8	K1 K8	KB1 KB8	KN1 KN8	KR1 KR8
QR2 QR7	QN2 QN7	QB2 QB7	Q2 Q7	K2 K7	KB2 KB7	KN2 KN7	KR2 KR7
QR3 QR6	QN3 QN6	QB3 QB6	Q3 Q6	K3 K6	KB3 KB6	KN3 KN6	KR3 KR6
QR4 QR5	QN4 QN5	QB4 QB5	Q4 Q5	K4 K5	KB4 KB5	KN4 KN5	KR4 KR5
QR5 QR4	QN5 QN4	QB5 QB4	Q5 Q4	K5 K4	KB5 KB4	KN5 KN4	KR5 KR4
QR6 QR3	QN6 QN3	QB6 QB3	Q6 Q3	K6 K3	KB6 KB3	KN6 KN3	KR6 KR3
QR7 QR2	QN7 QN2	QB7 QB2	Q7 Q2	K7 K2	KB7 KB2	KN7 KN2	KR7 KR2
QR8 QR1	QN8 QN1	QB8 QB1	Q8 Q1	K8 K1	KB8 KB1	KN8 KN1	KR8 KR1

The first letter of the tile name represents the side of the chessboard on which the tile is located. If it's on the queen's side, it starts with a Q. If it's on the King's side, it starts with a K. The second letter of the tile name represents the column. In descriptive notation, the columns are named after the piece that's positioned at the first rank for each particular column.

So, the first column to the left is "QR" meaning Queen's Rook, the second is "QN" (Queen's Knight), the third is "QB" (Queen's Bishop), and the fourth is just "Q" because it has the Queen on its first rank.

The number at the end represents the rank, just as it does in standard notation.

Let's take the example of the tile on the lower-left corner of the board in the image. You'll notice that it has QR8 and QR1 written in it, in dark and light colors respectively. The light QR1 means that the tile is "Queen's Rook 1" for the white player. The dark QR8 means that the tile is "Queen's Rook 8" for the black player.

In this notation, if the white player moves the Knight on QN1 to QR3, the move will be written down as Kt-QR3. If the black player made that exact move in those exact tiles, you'd have to use the black set of names to record it, so it would be completely different.

You can see why it's easier to use algebraic notation instead of descriptive notation. Still, as a beginner, descriptive notation helps you gain a deeper understanding of the chessboard layout.

Chapter 3: Chess Pieces and Their Movements

When playing chess, you are going to be dealing with just six unique pieces: The Pawn, the Knight, the Bishop, the Rook, the Queen, and the King. Each of these pieces has its own unique set of movements and abilities, which we are going to examine in this chapter.

The Pawn

We mentioned earlier that chess was designed to mimic the battlefield. Sticking with that metaphor, Pawns represent the infantry formation. They are on the frontlines in the fight. The white player starts with 8 Pawns on the second rank of the chessboard, while the black player starts out with 8 Pawns on the seventh rank. Pawns were traditionally seen as the least valuable pieces in the game. However, as modern rules and strategies emerged, they evolved into highly versatile pieces, and they can make a great impact on the game when skillfully used.

A Pawn moves one single space straight forward, as long as that space is not occupied by any other piece during that move. If a Pawn has not been moved at all in the game, it can move forward two spaces, provided both spaces are not occupied by another piece. A Pawn that has already been played at least once in the game cannot move two spaces.

A Pawn has the ability to capture any piece in the game by moving one single step diagonally. That means it can capture a piece in the forward left or the forward right direction. When it captures another piece, that piece will be removed from the board, and the Pawn will occupy that tile.

The following illustration shows a white Pawn moving in the forward right direction, (from d4 to e5) to capture a black Pawn on e5:

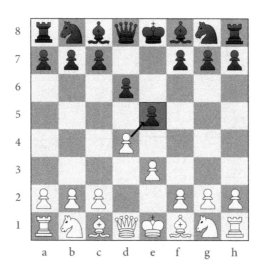

When the white player plays xe5, the black player could also play xe5 to capture the white Pawn.

En-passant

There is a special Pawn movement that's known as en-passant, which is French for "in passing." We will use the following image to explain this movement:

In the image, it is the white player's turn, and the black player has just moved their Pawn from e7 to e5. The white player is allowed to capture the black Pawn by moving the white Pawn on f5 to e6.

There are several things to note here. To start with, the white Pawn is on the fifth rank. A white Pawn can only capture a black Pawn en-passant if both Pawns are on the fifth rank, and they are right next to each other on either side. Similarly, a black Pawn can only capture a white Pawn en-passant when they are both on the fourth rank and are right next to each other in either direction.

This special rule was created because players used to take advantage of the two space movement allowance given to previously unmoved Pawns to escape a confrontation with the enemy Pawn. In the image, you'll notice that the black player could have moved the e7 Pawn to e6, which would put it at risk of capture by the white Pawn. The en-passant rule gives the white player the opportunity to even things by capturing the Pawn just as they could have done if the black player had played e6.

The en-passant capture is only allowed if the other player does it immediately after the two space Pawn movement has been done. If the white player makes a different move in the example above, they can't come back later to capture the black Pawn en-passant.

When a Pawn gets to the opposite end of a chessboard, it is immediately promoted to any other piece of the player's choosing, except for a King. For example, when a black Pawn reaches the first rank, the black player must choose to promote it to a Queen, Rook, Bishop, or Knight.

As you can see, Pawns can be very valuable, especially if they are well developed in the game and get to the other end of the board. Many chess games have been won because a player managed to get a Pawn promoted to a Queen. A promoted Pawn can be a game-changer.

One mistake most beginners make is to treat them as disposable. With the right strategy, and under certain conditions, a Pawn could end up being more valuable than a Knight or a Bishop.

As you learn to play your Pawns, think about how you can protect them to increase their chances of being promoted. Think about how you can develop them quickly so as to increase the chances of a quick Checkmate. Most importantly, keep your eyes on your opponent's Pawns, and never underestimate them.

The Knight

Sticking with our metaphor of a medieval battlefield, the Knight is the horse-riding Cavalry. It has the freedom and mobility to move around and help out at different sections of the battlefield as you make your advance. You can use it to block enemy pieces, clear blockages, and open up new battlefronts.

The Knight moves in a capital L shape. That means that it can move two steps in the horizontal direction and one step in the vertical direction, or it can move two steps in the vertical direction and one step in the horizontal direction. The Knight's movements are the most challenging to master, but once you get it, and as you play more and more, it will become intuitive.

The following illustration shows an example of a Knight's movement:

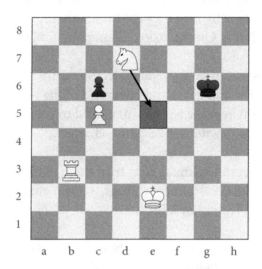

The white Knight on d7 moves to e5. That's two steps vertically downwards, and one space right in the horizontal direction. The Knight is a special piece in the sense that it's the only one that can jump over other pieces to get where it's going under all circumstances. It can skip over pieces of any color, irrespective of whether they are ally or opponent pieces. A Knight can capture any enemy piece that's positioned on a tile where it can legally land.

Due to their unique movement abilities, Knights are very valuable early in the game. Remember that each player starts out with a row full of Pawns on the front rank. This limits the mobility of the other powerful pieces on the back row, but Knights are the only ones that can jump over the Pawns and make headway into enemy territory in the first few moves.

Knights can also be used to cover a wide area, even on a heavily populated chessboard. Skilled players often try to position their Knights around the center of the chessboard early in the game so as to control that crucial region of the board. The following illustration shows the advantages of having a Knight around the center of the board:

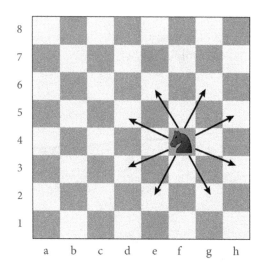

As you can see, the black Knight on f4 has the ability to land on 8 different squares, meaning it could capture any white pieces on those tiles.

The Bishop

The Bishop seems like an odd character to have on a battlefield, but it helps to think of it as a powerful authority figure with far-reaching influence. Some people equate the Bishop to archers on the battlefield, because once they get a clear line of vision to a target, they can strike from great distances with surgical precision.

Bishops move in straight diagonal lines over the board. They can move any number of spaces, as long as the path they are taking is clear at the moment. They can move in forward right, forward left, backward right, backward left directions as long as it's a straight diagonal. They can't jump over any pieces on the board but can capture any enemy piece on the tile where they land.

Because Bishops are restricted to diagonal movement, a Bishop that starts out on a black tile will only be able to move over and land on black tiles for the whole game. Similarly, a Bishop that's positioned on a white tile on the outside will only move along white tiles. The way the chessboard is set up, each player starts out with one Bishop on a white tile and one Bishop on a black tile.

Bishops are powerful pieces, but their abilities really shine through when the board has cleared a bit. That means that they are often quite limited during the opening. Take a look at the white Bishop in the following illustration:

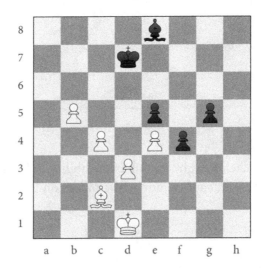

Here, the white Bishop on c2 is unable to get across the board and pose a threat to the black King because there is a blockage of Pawns around the center of the board. In order to put your Bishops into action, you need to clear a path for them so that they can navigate around the board.

When properly used, Bishops can be instrumental in executing long-range attacks that your opponent might not see coming.

The Rook

The Rook figurine looks like a castle. In fact, the Rook itself is sometimes referred to as a castle. However, in the battlefield metaphor, the Rook is often described as an armored chariot. That's fitting because the Rook is often used to protect the King during the late opening and early middle-game. After the Queen, the Rook is considered the second most powerful piece on the chessboard.

Rooks always move orthogonally, meaning parallel to the edges of the chessboard, in a straight line. They can move any number of spaces vertically or horizontally. However, they can never move diagonally.

The following illustration indicates the possible paths of movement for a Rook:

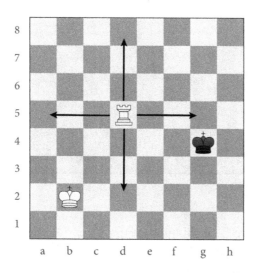

The white Rook on d5 can land on any tile along the paths indicated by the arrows, as long as the path is clear. The Rook can also capture any enemy piece on the paths indicated.

Rooks are often used to defend one's own King or to box in the opponent's King. Although they are very powerful pieces, Rooks are hard to deploy during the opening and in the early middle game because they are positioned on the corners of the chessboard. They often can't move horizontally because the whole first (or eighth) rank is full, and they are blocked by a Pawn in the vertical direction.

However, once the first rank has started to clear up, players have the opportunity to execute a special Rook and King move known as castling.

Castling

In the following diagram, the black player has the chance to play the castling move:

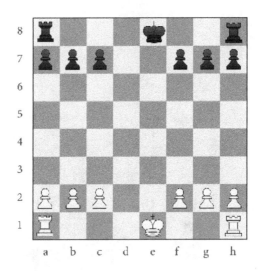

For a castling move to be legal, neither the King nor the Rook should have moved thus far in the game. Secondly, there shouldn't be any pieces between the King and the specific Rook with which the castling move is to be played. Assuming that the black player has not touched their King and the Rook on h8, they can castle by moving the King two spaces in the direction of the Rook, and then jumping the Rook over the King placing it in the space skipped by the King. The King will land on g8 and the Rook will land on f8 as shown in the image below:

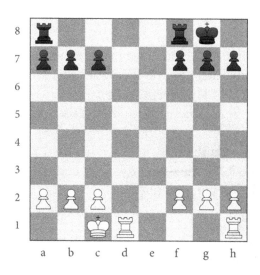

This specific instance of castling is known as "kingside castling" because the move is done with the King's Rook. Queenside castling is done the same way; the King moves two spaces in the direction of the Queen's Rook, and the Queen's Rook jumps over the King landing on the skipped space as shown for the white pieces in the image below:

For a castling move to be considered legal, there are several other conditions that need to be met. For starters, a player cannot use the castling move to get out of a Check. That means that if the King is in Check, during the move, it can't be castled.

Secondly, castling cannot be done through a tile that is in Check. If any of the tiles between the King and the Rook is covered by another piece (meaning it's on the path of a Queen, Bishop, Rook, Knight, or Pawn), then the King cannot skip it, and therefore cannot castle legally.

Finally, the King cannot land on a Check during castling. This means the move cannot be done if the tile where the King ends up is covered by an enemy piece as in the previous condition.

The Queen

The Queen is by far the most powerful piece on the chessboard and it's not known how and why the Queen ended up so powerful in the game. In older variations of the game, the Queen was known as the advisor, but even then, the piece didn't wield that much power. In any case, the Queen is the most versatile and most maneuverable piece you have at your disposal.

The Queen has the combined abilities of the Rook and the Bishop. That means that it can move both orthogonally and diagonally, any number of spaces, in all directions, as long as the path is clear.

The following illustration shows just how versatile a well-positioned Queen can be:

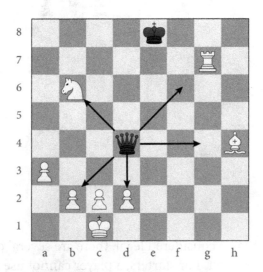

The black Queen on d4 can move in eight different directions, and it can capture any one of the pieces indicated in the image.

For beginners and masters alike, the Queen is often a crucial part of the winning strategy. Losing a Queen in the opening or middle-game can spell doom even for the most skilled players. Other players seek to bolster their chances of winning by advancing a Pawn to the end of the board and promoting it to a Queen.

The King

The chess King is something of a paradox. It is the weakest piece (arguably with the exception of the Pawn), yet at the same time, it's the one piece no one can afford to lose. Sticking with our medieval battle metaphor, the King is, well, the King. If the enemy captures your King, game over, you lose (although, usually, the game ends when it's clear that the King will be captured and there are no more legal moves to make, as we will discuss later).

The King can move only one space, but in any direction as long as the path is not blocked. The only exception to this rule is the castling move which we have discussed before. The King can capture any enemy piece that is right next to it in any direction.

Your primary objective while playing chess is to capture the enemy King before they capture your King. That means that every move you make in the game should ultimately be aimed at either protecting your King or pursuing your opponent's King.

PART 2: STRATEGIES FOR BEGINNERS

Chapter 4: Basic Principles

As I've mentioned, your objective as a player is to Checkmate the other player before they can Checkmate you. So the first principle of chess is understanding the concept of Checkmate. Checkmate occurs when one of the Kings on the board has been trapped in such a way that it is unable to make a legal move to another tile. The following illustration shows an example of a Checkmate:

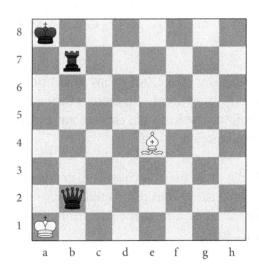

Here, the white King on a1 cannot move to a2 or b1, and it cannot capture the black Queen on b2 because of the black Rook on b7.

At this point in the game, the player whose King has been trapped loses the game. In the illustration, the black player wins, and the white player loses. So, when playing chess, everything you do – the plays you develop, the pieces you sacrifice, the attacks you launch – all of it should ultimately be in service of Checkmating the other King and protecting yours.

The next thing you need to understand is the concept of Check. In chess, Check is a situation where a King is under threat of being captured if the player doesn't intervene in their next move. The King is under threat but is still able to escape in one of two ways. The King can either move to a safe tile, or the player can use one of their other pieces to block the path of the piece that's threatening the King or capture it.

The following illustration shows an example of a King that's in Check:

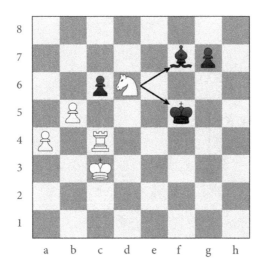

Here, the white Knight on d6 has put the black King on f5 on Check. It's the black player's move, and they have no choice but to move their King.

The scenario in the illustration also demonstrates the benefit of putting the other player on Check (and the perils of having your own King Checked). The white Knight also threatens to capture the Bishop on f7. Since the black player must prioritize saving their King, they cannot move the Bishop, so the white Knight will have an easy time capturing it. The point is, putting another player in Check is a very effective way of forcing them to make trades that disadvantage them and benefit you.

Draws In Chess

Now that you understand Checks and Checkmates, you know that a game of chess can end in a win or a loss. There is however a third outcome in chess – a draw.

The first and most common kind of draw in chess is the stalemate. A stalemate is said to happen when a player who is not in Check has no legal move to make when it's their turn to play. When a stalemate happens, the game ends immediately, and it's considered a draw. The following illustration shows a stalemate scenario:

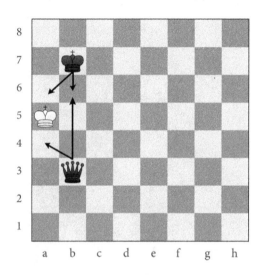

At first glance, it may appear as though the black player is headed for a win, but that's not the case. The white King on a5 is not currently in Check. It's the white player's turn to move, but as you can see, they can't make any move without putting themselves in Check. This game will end at this point as a draw.

In the endgame, if you are at a disadvantage, you can try to force the other player into a stalemate draw to avoid losing altogether. If the shoe is on the other foot and you have an advantage and are likely to win, you need to be careful as you attempt to trap your opponent so as to avoid a stalemate draw.

There are other kinds of draws in chess, but they are very rare. They include:

The threefold repetition rule – If the same position is repeated three separate times in the game (i.e. all the pieces are exactly where they were on the board two times before), a player can claim a draw. This rule is meant to put an ending to a game that seems to be stuck in some kind of loop. The idea is that if the players keep on playing the game, they'll end up right where they are over and over. In professional chess matches, an arbiter is brought in to determine whether the conditions for the rule have been met.

The fifty move rule – if each player makes fifty moves (for a total of 100 consecutive moves) and no Pawn movement or piece capture occurs in that span, the game ends in a draw.

A draw also occurs in situations where it's clear that Checkmate is unattainable for both players.

Finally, a draw may occur at any point during the game if one player offers a draw, and the other one obliges. When one player offers a draw, it's completely up to the other one to accept or turn it down – a player cannot be coerced into a draw.

Relative Value Of Chess Pieces

Chess pieces are not created equal. Given what you know so far, I bet you'd agree that you would rather lose a Pawn than a Queen in most scenarios during the game. As you've seen, each piece has different abilities, and ideally, during your campaign, you would want to capture your opponent's powerful pieces and retain your powerful pieces. Along the way, you are going to be faced with lots of strategic decisions, like; "Should I sacrifice my Rook so that I can capture their Bishop?" or "Should I let them capture my Knight so that I can have a shot at their Queen?"

It's decisions like these that make it important to understand the relative value of chess pieces. It is difficult to assign a value to a piece because the usefulness of each piece varies, not just from one game to the next, but also within the same game. For instance, you can say that a Knight is more valuable than a Pawn. But what about if the Pawn has just one single step to get to the other side of the board, and has a clear path to promotion?

Chess scholars disagree on the relative value of chess pieces, but for education purposes, the standard values assigned to chess pieces are as follows:

Pawn - 1
Knight - 3
Bishop - 3
Rook - 5
Queen - 9
King - Priceless

These values are assumed to apply to the pieces at the start of the game. As the game goes on, some pieces may become more valuable, and others may become less valuable.

It's worth emphasizing that these values are not set in stone. Chess matches are very complex, and they can take any direction. However, the numbers can come in handy when you are trying to make a decision along the way. A Rook has a value of 5 while a Bishop has a value of 3. So, it may not be wise to sacrifice your Rook to capture your enemy's Bishop. However, even that depends on the specific scenario; it might be that you still have an advantage after losing your Rook and that capturing the enemy Bishop is a stepping stone to a Checkmate.

The point is that relative values are just meant as a general guide, and you will have to use your own judgment in each instance.

Chapter 5: Opening Strategies

The opening refers to the first stage of any chess match. As a beginner, you need to understand that the opening sets the tone for the whole game. Those first few moves you make are very important in determining the advantages you'll gain throughout the game, and whether or not you'll end up winning. Some beginners have a tendency to hold back for fear of exposing their King, instead of taking advantage of the opening stage to develop their own pieces. In this chapter, we'll look at strategies that you can use and mistakes that you should avoid in the opening.

In the opening, your main objective is to develop your pieces as fast as possible, so that you can get them into play. So, in the first few moves you make, the optimal strategy is to play the pieces that open paths for the development of other pieces. For each player, the front line is full of Pawns, so the first move you make can only be a Pawn or a Knight.

Given these criteria, the best first move for either player, in theory, would be to play d4 or e4. That's because these moves immediately put a Bishop and a Queen into play. The d4 move is known as the Queen's Pawn opening, and the e4 move is known as the King's Pawn opening.

The King's Pawn Opening

Statistically, this is the single most popular white player opening in professional chess. The following diagram illustrates why that's the case:

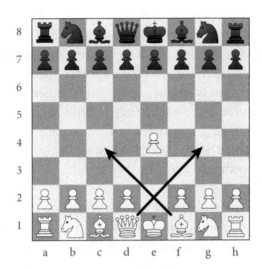

As you can see, playing e4 clears the path for the white player to move both the Queen and the Bishop in subsequent moves. For a beginner, this move is going to appear counterintuitive. From what you've learned so far, the whole point of the game is to protect your King and capture the other King. Moving the King's Pawn makes your King feel naked. However, this early in the game, you can quickly make good development moves that will leave your King adequately protected.

Statistically, the c5 move is the most common answer by the black player to the King's Pawn opening. This move is referred to as the Sicilian defense. The move puts the black player's Queen into action, but as you can see, it doesn't open up as many development opportunities as the white opening. This explains why the white player is believed to have a slight first-mover advantage at the start of the chess match.

The Ruy Lopez Opening, depicted in the following illustration, is one of the best examples of how quickly a game can develop given a King's Pawn opening:

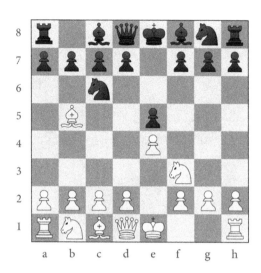

The moves are as follows:

1. e4 e5
2. Nf3 Nc6
3. Bb5…

In just three moves, the white player already has a Knight and Bishop out and about on the board, while the black player has a Knight and can deploy the Queen on the next move.

The point of this example is that you don't have to restrict yourself to just a series of Pawn movements during the opening.

The Queen's Pawn Opening

The d4 move is often used when the white player is trying to develop the Queen's Bishop and to potentially pull off a queenside castling move. The following board shows one common way in which this opening tends to play out:

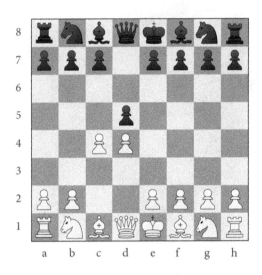

The moves are as follows:

1. d4 d5
2. c4...

Here, the black player counters the opening with d5, and in response, white offers another Pawn with the c4 play. This is known as the Queen's gambit. The black player has a tough choice to make. They can take the Pawn with dxc4, but this would allow the white player to take dominion over the center area of the board. This opening sequence was very popular in the 20th century, and you'll encounter it many times if you study classic chess games. We will take a deeper look at the Queen's gambit in Chapter 7, after we have discussed center control techniques.

Rules & Principles For A Good Opening

There are some key principles that you need to keep in mind during the opening. We will illustrate these principles using examples.

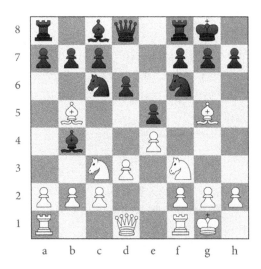

The following sequence of play was followed to arrive at the game shown in the illustration above:

1. e4 e5
2. Nf3 Nc6

Up to this point, you see that both players have opened paths for their stronger pieces, and they have used their Knights to defend their respective King's Pawns so as to avoid ceding control of the center of the board to the other.

3. Nc3 Nf6

On this move, both have chosen to develop their own Knights and put them into play.

4. Bb5 Bb4

Here, they have brought out their Bishops correctly, after the Knights have already taken a strong position at the center of the board.

5. 0-0 0-0

Here, they each have moved to castle their Kings.

6. d3 d6

Here, both players have cleared a path to put their Queens and queenside Bishops in play. So far, you can see that the two players have been making similar moves, but at this point, the game transitions from the opening to the middle game.

7. Bg5 Bxc3

As a beginner, there are some things you can learn from this game. First, notice that each player has been able to develop the game in just seven steps. This has been achieved in part because no one has moved any piece more than once throughout the development process. The principle to internalize here is that you shouldn't move your pieces more than once during development, unless you stand to gain something important, such as freedom of action, or some kind of material advantage. In other words, don't waste your moves, make them count.

Another thing to notice from the game is that each player chose repeatedly to move other pieces instead of Pawns. Moving Pawns in the opening may seem like an easy choice, but it will put you at a disadvantage if you are playing against someone who has a bit more experience.

The third thing you should notice is that the players developed their Knights and Bishops before their Rooks and Queens. If you recall the relative values of the pieces, the Rooks and the Queen are more valuable than the Knights and Bishops, so you really want to avoid a scenario where you lose one of those pieces that early in the game. Knights and Bishops offer the best balance in terms of risk and reward in the opening stage of the game. However, it's okay to bring out a Queen or Rook early if you see a quick path to a Checkmate, or if you are forced to defend your King.

An additional principle to remember is that you should bring out at least one Knight before you put either one of your Bishops in play. When the board is crowded, Bishops tend to have limited mobility, and they can be easily captured by enemy Pawns if they aren't well covered. Knights can provide the protection that Bishops need to prevent early capture.

Fool's Mate

In the following figure, you'll see a common mistake that beginner chess players make which could lead to a Checkmate in just two moves. It's called a fool's mate.

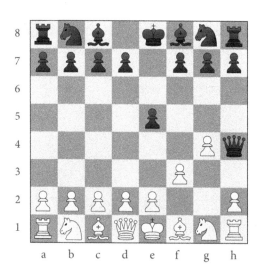

The play sequence is as follows:

1. f3 e5
2. g4 Qh4#

Here, the white player makes the mistake of moving Pawns on one side of the board, perhaps in the hope of creating a blockage. However, the enemy Queen is able to swoop in and Checkmate them immediately. This is the fastest possible win in a game of chess, and it's often used to illustrate why playing Pawns and "saving" powerful pieces is a bad strategy in chess.

There are lots of other principles and strategies that come in handy during the opening, but you need to master the ones we have discussed here so far so you can have a solid foundation for more complex strategies. Remember that although good openings don't necessarily guarantee wins, mistakes made on the opening stage can be dire, and are very difficult to recover from.

Chapter 6: Taking Control Of The Center

Tiles d4, e4, d5, and e5 make up a four-square grid that is the center of the chessboard. These tiles are of strategic importance in the middle-game, so you need to try and take control of them as part of your late opening strategy. Chess scholars have found that a violent attack strategy is not possible if a player doesn't control at least two of those four squares. So, as you develop your Knights, Bishops, and Pawns in your first few moves, try to consider how you can use that at that point to take control of the center.

Consider the following series of moves:

1. e4 e5
2. Nf3 d6
3. d4 Nd7
4. Bc4 h6
5. Nc3 Nf6
6. Be3 Be7
7. Qe2 c6
8. Rd1 Qc7
9. 0-0

When the white player makes the ninth move, the board looks like this:

In the first two moves, you see that while the white player is developing their Knight, the black player seems to be taking a defensive approach by playing a second Pawn when they don't need to. By the third move, the white player starts a fight for control of the center, and the black player refuses to give it up and responds by bringing out a Knight. Still, the black player makes an error. They use the Knight to protect their Pawn on e5, but in the process, they block their Bishop and Queen.

From these moves, you can see that the moment the game starts, the race for control of the center starts with it. Any unnecessary Pawn movements will set you back, as it did with the black player when they made the d6 move.

Another thing worth noting is that the white player holds off on castling until they have developed their pieces and they have a solid control of the center. That's something else to keep in mind. If you are too focused on castling during your opening, you may lose crucial moves and allow the other player to develop into the center, and that would be a great disadvantage.

At this point in the game, you can see that the white player has finished their development (meaning most of their pieces are free to move) while the black player is hampered. To take control of the center, you must adhere to the principles of a good opening strategy.

There are other strategies where the player doesn't seek to control the center. One such strategy is called flanking, and it involves shoring up the pieces to the sides of the board so as to launch an attack from one or both sides. Even with such a strategy, it's important to remember to prefer piece movements over Pawn movements whenever it's possible.

Chapter 7: The Queen's Gambit

The queen's gambit starts with the moves:
1. d4 d5
2. c4…

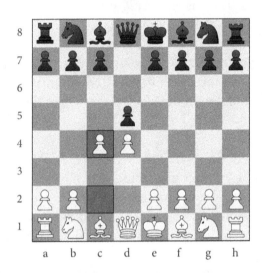

When the white player offers the Queen's gambit, it means that they give away a Pawn early in the game. It's a gambit (a gamble) because the black player has to accept the Pawn offer for the strategy to play out. If black plays dxc4, white can play e4 and immediately have two Pawns at the center of the board as shown in the figure below.

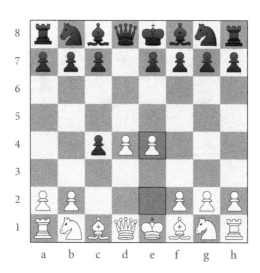

Notice that although the white player is down one Pawn, they might be able to even things out by playing Bxc4 if the black Pawn remains undefended in the next few moves. Still, the positional advantage of having control of the center early in the opening may be worth losing a Pawn.

Queen's Gambit Accepted

When the black player follows the white's second move, c4 with dxc4, that play is called "Queen's gambit accepted." In such a case, the black player lets the white player have a chance at controlling the center of the board, but they will likely move to defend the Pawn on c4, for example, by playing b5 in a subsequent move.

If the black player launches this defense, there are two general ways that the white player can proceed. First, they can undermine black's defense of their Pawn, as shown in the following move:

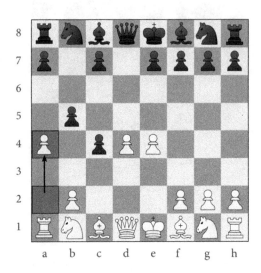

By using the Pawns on files "a" and "b" the white player can keep dismantling any Pawn formations that the black player may set up. If for example, from this image, the black player plays a6, the white player can go right ahead and play axb5. It's unlikely the black player will counter with axb5 because that would leave their a8 Rook exposed. Ultimately, the white player will be able to level things out by capturing one black Pawn.

The second way that the white player can proceed (after the black player defends their c4 Pawn with the b5 move), is to just ignore the defense and to keep developing their own pieces. They can bring out both of their Knights and keep strengthening their position in the center. If the black player uses more than one of their opening moves defending just one Pawn, and the white player continues developing, the black player might fall back significantly and enter the middlegame with a weak setup.

Queen's Gambit Declined

When the white player offers the Pawn with the c4 move, and the black player doesn't take it, instead choosing to protect their claim to the center with the e6 move, this play is called "Queen's gambit declined."

The Queen's gambit declined is one of the most legendary openings in professional chess. It gives the black player room to quickly develop their King's side minor pieces (Knight and Bishop) and do a kingside castle. Notice from the image that the black Bishop on f8 has a clear path across the board, and can even Check the white King with a Bb4 play.

If you are the white player, the best way to proceed from a Queen's gambit decline would be to bring out your Knights and to keep developing your c1 Bishop.

In the following image, you can see how the Queen's gambit decline can play out:

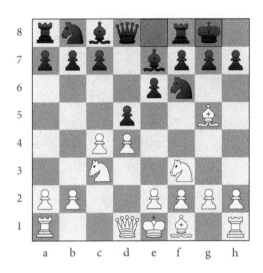

The black player has managed to fortress their King. The white player used the Nc3 move to cover their King, and can now mobilize their Queen, together with the Bishop now on g5 to try and dismantle the fortress. At this point, the white player still has the chance to castle either kingside or queenside, although they have to weigh that option against the chance to infiltrate the black player's fortress before the black player can mobilize their queenside pieces. The infiltration option is very advanced, so as a beginner, the more sensible thing to do would be to seek positional gains while at the same time trying to pull off the castling move. A kingside castle for the white player might be a better option because they still have a solid Pawn formation there.

The Slav Defense

The Slav defense is another way for the black player to turn down the Queen's gambit. The difference between the Slav defense and the Queen's gambit declined is that the black player defends their d5 Pawn with a c6 play instead of e6. The Slav defense is shown in the following image:

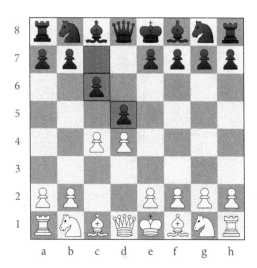

In the Slav defense, the black player opens a development path for their c8 Bishop, but in the process, they block their b8 Knight. If you are the white player in this case, you should keep developing your pieces following general chess principles; bring out your Knights first and keep seeking out positional gains.

One thing that could give you an advantage, as a beginner in this progression, would be to play Qb3 after bringing out your Knights, as shown in the following image:

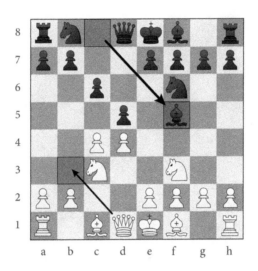

If the black player develops their Bishop as indicated, you can then play Qxb7. This would work if you are up against another beginner, but an opponent who has been around the block would see it coming and take action to prevent it.

Dealing With Other Defenses To The Queen's Gambit

Once you have offered the Queen's gambit as the white player, your opponent may make different moves apart from a Pawn defense. Let's look at how you can proceed in such cases.

In the following image, the black player defends with a Knight move:

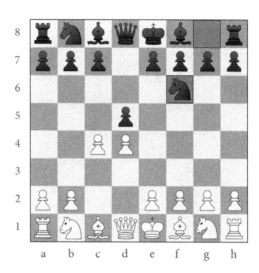

Here, the way for the white player to proceed would be to capture the black Pawn with the cxd5 move. If there is no Pawn on c6 or e6, only the black Knight or Queen can capture the white d5 Pawn in response to this move. If black plays Nxd5, proceed to take over the center as shown in the following image:

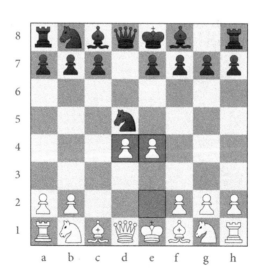

If they play Qxd5, you can start bringing out your Knights to push back against their Queen and preserve your claim to the center, as shown in the image below:

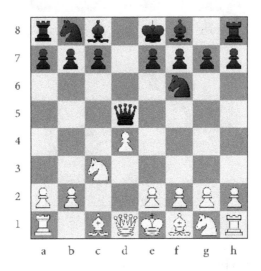

As you have seen so far, based on the progressions we have looked at, the Queen's gambit is a very solid opening strategy, and mastering it can significantly improve your game even as a beginner.

The only time the Queen's gambit is really threatened is when the black player counters with other gambits. For example, they could play the Albin counter gambit which is shown in the following image:

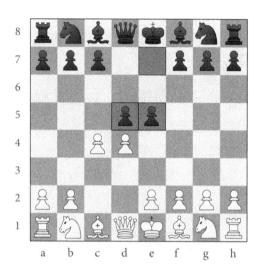

Here, after offering the Queen's gambit, the black player responds with their own gambit by playing e5. For the white player, this poses a real danger of losing the center. If white plays cxd5 and black plays Qxd5, black now has two center squares and can inhibit white's development. Even if different moves are made here, black still has a real chance of taking root at the center and developing quickly.

To prevent the black player from posing the Albin counter gambit, sometimes the white player can play Nf3 on the second move before offering the queen's gambit in the third move. There are several techniques that can be used to fight the Albin counter gambit, but they require advanced knowledge of chess theory. As a beginner, if you are faced with the counter gambit and you haven't prepared with the Knight move, just remember the fundamental chess principles and keep developing your pieces. You'll still fare very well, and you might even be able to take back the center.

Dealing With The Queen's Gambit As The Black Player

When you are offered the Queen's gambit by the white player, you can accept it. That in itself is not a bad move, but you are taking on a bit of risk, and you need to know what you are doing. Here is the Queen's gambit from the perspective of the black player:

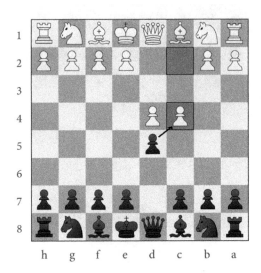

Should you choose to accept the gambit, you need to move fast so that you don't lose the center. We've seen that the white player will most likely move into a second center tile by playing e4, so you need to counter that.

One way to do that is by playing e5 as shown in the following image:

Here, even though the white player has two center squares, you can fight against it as follows: if white plays Bxc4, you can take the center Pawn with exd4. If instead the white player chooses to take your Pawn with dxe5, that's fine too because both of your Queen's are exposed, and you can pull off an early Queen trade. That means that you play Qxd1+ and the white King takes your Queen as well with Kxd1. If both Queen's are cleared from the board, it can be a good thing for you because, first, you are even on that count, and second, you can develop your pieces a lot faster without the looming threat of a versatile enemy Queen. If the Queen trade occurs, you have a shot at an aggressive play. You can play Nc6 to exert some control around the center, and you can even follow that with Bg4+ to put the white King in Check, which might throw them off their game.

After you've accepted the Queen's gambit, the white player may play Nf3 instead of immediately moving to increase their Pawns at the center. The move is shown in the following diagram:

As you can see, playing e5 is no longer a good move for black. In this case, you should bring out your Knight with Nf6 to protect the center, then develop your c8 Bishop. You can then open up your other Bishop by playing e6 and this is how the board will look:

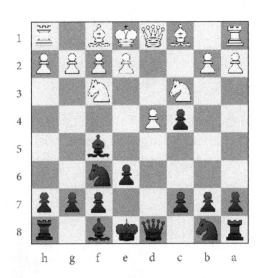

If you keep developing your minor pieces, you might be able to pull off a queenside castle and have fully developed pieces by the middlegame despite the white player's countermoves.

Black Player's Queen's Gambit Declined

In case you choose to decline the gambit, the most likely scenario is that the white player will still want to develop into the center, so bring out your Knight with the Nf6 move.

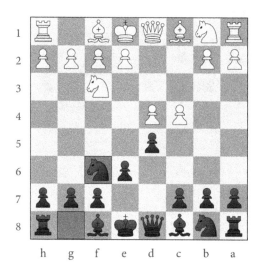

You still have your d5 Pawn at risk if the white player doesn't move to capture it on the third move. It is okay to bolster its defense, but you shouldn't do that at the expense of developing your pieces. If possible, make moves that are both developing and defensive. If you choose to develop your Bishop on f8, do so knowing that you might have to trade it for one of the enemy pieces on the queenside. This move gives you the best chance to castle on the kingside.

Chigorin Defense

There is another strategy called the Chigorin defense which you can use in response to the offer of a Queen's gambit. Here, your strategy would be to get your Queen at the center of the board. To do this, you should follow the Queen's gambit with Nc6 as shown in the following image.

In this setup, if white plays cxd5, you play Qxd5. You can then proceed to strengthen your position at the center with e5. You can then develop your other pieces while protecting your Queen as shown in the following diagram:

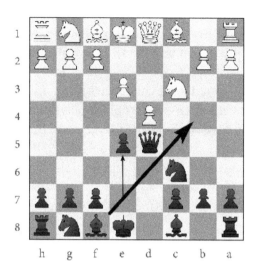

As you can see here, the white player brings in their Knight with the Nc3 move to try and flush out your Queen, but by playing Bb4, you can pin down their Knight by threatening their King should they move the Knight.

Playing The Queen's Gambit As A Beginner

The Queen's gambit will serve you well as a beginner before you can start figuring out more complex strategies. As I've mentioned, even professional's still use this opening quite regularly, so keep studying it and understand all the variations that we have looked at here, and any other that you may come across. Another thing to note is that you shouldn't be rigid when using the Queen's gambit. If your opponent changes the game, adapt your strategy to the new conditions. Many beginners come into the game with set expectations on how the opening ought to play out, so when they are faced with an opponent who doesn't allow them to roll out a clean Queen's gambit, they get thrown off balance. My advice is that you should master the strategy but always retain your ability to think on your feet.

Chapter 8: The King's Indian Defense

The King's Indian Defense is one of the most popular chess openings for the black player, but it can also be used by the white player. The point of this defense is to secure the King in the opening before making any further moves. It gives black a decent chance to win against the Queen's Pawn opening, which is why it's often used by black players even in the highest levels of play. No matter what the white player does, the black player can use the King's Indian Defense by playing d6, Nf6, g6, Bg7, and then castle on the King's side. This keeps the King safe until the game develops further.

The image below shows a proper King's Indian setup before the King and Rook have castled:

The King's Indian is a hyper-modern style of playing chess. It is a great strategy to study for beginners because it goes against the conventional wisdom that you need to have pieces at the center of the board in order to have control over the game.

So far, we have looked at the benefits of controlling the center and the Queen's gambit which is essentially a battle for the center. However, with the King's Indian, we have a beginner strategy that allows a player to fare well in the game despite relinquishing control over the center to their opponent early in the game.

In the image, you can see that by the end of the fourth move, the white player has Pawns on c4, d4, and e4. They have pieces on two of the center squares, and can immediately capture any piece that moves to the other two center squares. Additionally, they already have a Knight flanking the Pawns for extra protection. The King's Indian is a strategy that the black player can use to defend against this onslaught.

If you look at the black player's King side formation, you'll notice that they are limited to the sixth rank because of the white Queen and Bishop, so they can't make an advance to the fifth rank. So, to develop, the black player would have to start Pawn advances either at the center or on the queenside, and even then, the movements are very restricted. If you are an aggressive player, playing this strategy as the black player won't feel right for you. You are mostly going to be making moves in response to what the white player does, and it can be unnerving if you prefer to be the one controlling the action.

There are several variations on how the King's Indian plays out. Let's now look at some of the most common ones.

The Averbakh Variation

In one variation, the white player proceeds from the setup in the image above by playing Be2. Black will respond by castling as shown in the following diagram, and white will bring out their other Bishop with the Bg5 move:

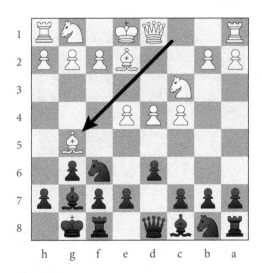

For black, the play is straightforward. Now that they have built a strong defensive fortress around their King, they can now make a slow but deliberate push on the queenside. By playing c5, black starts applying pressure on the white player who doesn't want to lose control over the center by breaking their wall of Pawns. This move still forces the white player to act. They can capture the Pawn, but more often than not, white is likely to respond to this by playing d5. Either way, the black player manages to weaken the white player's stranglehold over the center.

The next play for black would be to bring their queenside Knight to further break apart white's center control. They can do so as shown in the following diagram:

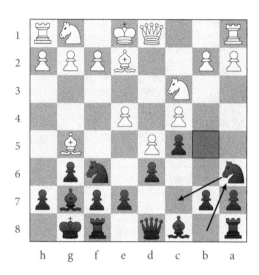

It will take the black player several moves to advance their Knight without blocking the path for the Bishop on c8. Alternatively, they can carefully advance their two Pawns on a7 and b7 while making sure that they protect each other, or are well covered by the Rook on a8. The black player would have to keep being aggressive on the queenside, possibly offering some trades as they advance, but they will remain passive and reactive on the Kings side where they will try to maintain the fortress until the middle-game.

The Classical Variation

In this variation, the white player starts from the King's Indian setup by bringing out their kingside Knight first instead of their Bishops, as shown in the following diagram:

White plays Nf3. This is a very expected move, especially for a white player that adheres to the basic principles of a good opening. They focus on developing their pieces, and are keen on preceding with the Knight before the Bishop.

The logical response for the black player would be to castle kingside (just like in the previous variation). White will then play Be2, perhaps also with the intention of castling on the kingside. Black follows this by playing e5, starting to pressure white's Pawns at the center.

White now castles on the King's side, and black brings their Knight out with Nc3.

Here, you start to see a clear difference between the classical variation and the Averbakh variation. With the Knight move, the black player is setting to push forward through the center in the classic variation. Recall that in the Averbakh variation, the push is mostly done towards the far end of the queenside.

You have to keep in mind which variation of the King's Indian Defense you are playing when you move to protect your Knights. If you are trying to save your Knight from capture, make sure you do it in a way that does the least damage to the play that you have chosen. If you are pushing forward through the central files of the board, you want to retreat your Knights in a way that still allows you to have control over those central files. Similarly, if you are pushing forward on the queenside, ensure you retreat your Knight without making it harder for you to resume your push.

Let's take the following image as an example:

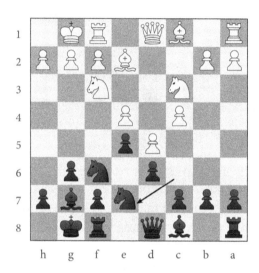

In this classical variation, the black player sets up their Knight first on c6 to put pressure on the e4 Pawn, because they want to advance through the center. If they are pressured to pull back, they are better off playing Ne7 instead of Na5. At the e7 tile, they can still apply pressure on the white Pawn and can be part of another structure on the same region of the board.

The Samisch Variation

In this variation, white starts with f3, as shown in the following diagram:

Once the white player makes this move, the black player can learn a few things. First, that white intends to make an aggressive attack on the King's side. Second, that white probably intends to castle on the queen's side.

Black will castle on the kingside, and prepare to launch an aggressive attack on the queenside where the white player will be positioning their King. To put the King in position, white will start by clearing out the Bishop, probably by playing Be3. Here, black is presented with an opportunity to poke a hole in the wall of white Pawns at the center.

As you can see in the diagram, black can offer a Pawn with the c5 play. This could play out a couple of different ways. If white takes the Pawn, it could lead to a Queen trade that would prevent the white player from fortressing their King. If white doesn't take the Pawn, the black player will gain significant material and a positional advantage.

For a beginner, one thing you can take away from the King's Indian Defense is that control over the center is just the beginning of the battle in a game of chess. This is especially important to remember when you are playing black because the white player's first mover advantage can help them take to the center a lot faster than you. Keep practicing all the three King's Indian defenses that we have discussed in this chapter so that you have the skills you need to push back against even the most formidable white player.

Chapter 9: Middle-Game Strategies

Ideally, the middlegame starts when the players have developed their pieces. Compared to openings and endgames, middlegames are the least studied parts of chess matches. This is because there are so many variables at play during this stage, which makes it difficult to single out specific scenarios that are of importance to future players. Still, there are certain general rules and principles which you need to understand in order to get the best out of your middlegame.

Your ultimate goal in the middlegame would be, of course, to Checkmate your opponent, but there are several smaller goals that you might need to accomplish in the middlegame to make that possible. Sometimes, Checkmates may occur drastically in the middlegame (or even in the opening), but in most cases, when you are dealing with two players of matched abilities, the middlegame will keep progressing until that game goes into the endgame.

There are two main things that you will be trying to do in the middlegame. First, you'll try to gain a material advantage, meaning you will want to capture your enemy's pieces while keeping your pieces from being captured. Second, you will try to gain strategic advantages, meaning that you will attempt to take control of crucial positions on the board, pin down your enemy's pieces, keep advancing your own pieces, etc.

One mistake that most beginners make in the middle game is waiting around for the other player to make an error so that they can gain some advantage. From your very first chess game, try to avoid this mindset. Instead, think of ways that you can coordinate your own pieces and launch an attack on your enemy before they can launch an attack on you, or before they can set up a formidable defense.

You need to create your own advantages, and you can do this in a number of ways. First, you can take the initiative to control the tempo or timing of the game. Make moves that force the other player to be reactive, try to avoid a situation where the other player is the one forcing you to react. You can also try to gain a space advantage over your opponent. The player whose pieces are crammed together has a disadvantage of navigating the chessboard during the middlegame, but if your pieces are spaced out, you'll have more room to maneuver. You can also seek to control certain sections of the board, whether it's kingside, queenside, or the center.

Pawn Strategies In The Middlegame

To gain an advantage in the middlegame, you can create strong Pawn structures to increase the chances of Pawn promotion towards the end-game, and to hold on to important positions on the board. Isolated Pawns can get picked off easily by enemy pieces, but well-structured clusters of Pawns can protect each other, so try to create superior Pawn structures whenever you can.

The following image illustrates weak Pawn structures that you want to avoid:

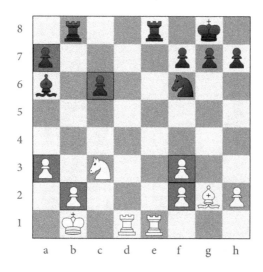

Both players have some weak Pawn structures in this case. Doubled Pawns like the ones on f2 and f3 don't have much maneuverability, and they can be captured without a trade. The black Pawn on c6 is isolated. Both players have traded their middle Pawns and are mostly left with flanked Pawns. As a general rule, you should try to retain your middle Pawns because they are slightly more valuable than the ones on the sides. If you can, trade your flanked Pawns with your opponent's middle Pawn so that you can gain or retain strategic control of the center.

Protecting The King In The Middlegame

The middlegame is an especially dangerous time for your King because with a fully developed board, you may fail to see an attack coming, and you could lose the game in an instant. To avoid this, you need to position your King strategically so that he is protected from unforeseen attacks. You also want to be careful not to overextend your pieces while pursuing the enemy King to the point where you thin out your own defense and leave your King vulnerable.

The ideal positioning for a King during the middlegame involves having it protected, first by an impenetrable Pawn formation. Additionally, you need to have some of your pieces positioned in such a way that they can fall back and come to the King's aid immediately if your opponent poses a threat.

The castling move that we discussed early in the book is one of the most effective defense strategies for a King.

In this illustration, you can see that both players have castled their Kings behind fortresses of Pawns and other pieces. In this case, if either one of them tries to go for a quick Checkmate in the middlegame, the other one will see it coming.

When creating a defensive position for your King, you want to make sure that you don't leave any weak tiles within or near your defensive position. Such weak squares can allow your opponent to move in and hold the position, which will turn out to be an outpost that they can use to design an attack.

Take the following image as an example:

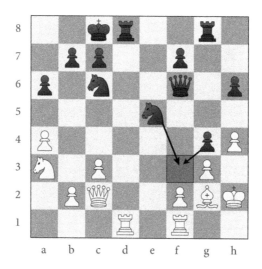

Tile f3 is a weak square for the white player because it can be infiltrated by the black Knight on e5, which will put the white King in Check. This is very risky in the middlegame.

Earlier in the book, we looked at the values of different pieces, and how you can decide whether or not to sacrifice or risk a certain piece in order to capture an enemy piece. In the middlegame, this gets more complicated because there are times when you will have to weigh the value of some pieces against positions on the board. For example, would you be willing to sacrifice a Knight in order to take or retain control over the center of the board? Some chess players tend to value material (i.e. chess pieces) over position, while the reverse is true for other players.

When the middlegame transitions into the endgame, you should take stock of whether you are at an advantage or a disadvantage. Ideally, you should move into the next stage with a well-protected King, with well-positioned pieces, and with a material advantage over your opponent. If you have managed to gain this lead, you will have to focus on using it to crush your opponent in the endgame. If you come out less dominant in the middle-game, you may find that your opponent has an easy time forcing you on the defensive, and in the worst circumstances, you might find that your best shot is to try and force a draw.

Chapter 10: Endgame Strategies

In the endgame, most of the chessboard would have cleared and each player would have anywhere from one to a handful of pieces besides the King (note that in the strictest technical sense, Pawns aren't considered pieces). This is the culmination of all that you have been working towards – if your middlegame went the right way, you will only have your most favored pieces at this stage, or you will have dominion over your favored territories. Now, you have to embark on an unrelenting hunt of your opponent's King, and do everything you can to corner it. Some endgames are quick while others are drawn out.

Here, we are going to look at common end game scenarios, with and without Pawns. We will look at the best and fastest way to trap your opponent's King without risking a draw.

Scenario 1: King & Rook Vs King

One way to win in such a scenario is by driving the opposing King to one side of the chessboard and limiting its movement to that rank or file before slowly closing in.

Consider the example in the following illustration, where its white's turn to move:

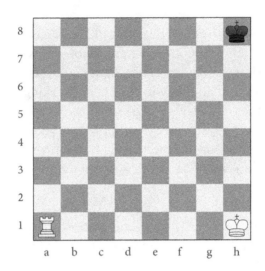

Here, the white player can win by first moving the Rook to a7. That way, the black King will be restricted to the eight rank, because the seventh rank is Checked. The black King will move to g8. In response, the white player should move their King to g2. The principle that the white player needs to follow in this case is to try as much as possible to ensure that their King stays on the same file as the black King. If the black King were trapped in a file instead of a rank, then the white player would have to ensure that their King stayed on the same rank as the black King.

The white player should follow this pattern until their King arrives at the fifth rank (i.e. until there are two ranks left between the two kings. As they proceed to the sixth rank, instead of placing the white King on the same file as the black one, the white player should move to the file next to the one the black King is on in order to prevent the black King from changing direction and start moving back where it came from.

As shown in the following image, upon reaching the fifth rank, the white King moves to d6 and not c6. That way, the black King cannot retreat to d8.

From this point on, the white player can Checkmate the black King with the following moves:

1. Kd6 Kb8
2. Rc7 Ka8
3. Kc6 Kb8
4. Kb6 Ka8
5. Rc8#

In the following example, the black King starts out at the center of the board:

Here, the correct approach for the white player would be to use both of their pieces to reduce the mobility of the black King and trap it. First, they should advance their King towards the center of the board. The black King will move away from the center in one direction or another. The white player should in turn use their Rook to create a boundary past which the black King can no longer move.

In this illustration, the Rook on the fifth rank ensures that the black King is no longer able to move to the top half of the board. If the black King moves to c3, the white Rook should move to h4 to limit its mobility further. If on the other hand, the black King moves to b4, the white King should pursue it by moving to d3. The point is to continuously confine the black King to fewer squares, until it is Checkmated.

You'll notice that the white player is able to keep the Rook from being captured by carefully moving their King right next to it in the final attack. For beginners, such a move can require practice to master, so set it up on a board and practice over and over so that you fully understand the thought process behind each move.

Scenario 2: King & Queen Vs King

You now know that the Queen has the combined powers of the Rook and Bishop, which means that this should be a fairly easy Checkmate to pull off. The game can proceed as follows:

1. Qc6 Kd4
2. Kd2 Ke5
3. Ke3 Kf5
4. Qd6 Kg5
5. Qe6 Kh4
6. Qg6 Kh3
7. Kf3 Kh4

8.   Qg4#

Scenario 3: Two Bishops & King Vs King

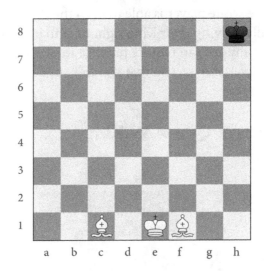

In this case, the white player is able to win by driving the black King to the edge of the board and trapping it in a corner without risking a stalemate.

The game can proceed as follows:

1.   Bd3 Kg7
2.   Bg5 Kf7
3.   Bf5 Kg7
4.   Kf2 ...

At this point, the black King will be trapped in a 5 tile area. Unless one of the Bishops is moved, the black King can only move there. However, as long as it has safe tiles, the game can't go into a stalemate.

The white King has to be brought up to the sixth rank and has to be placed on g6, h6, f7, or f8 so that the black King can be pinned into the corner. The white player would have to mark time for a few turns before they get the chance to completely Checkmate the black King.

The rest of the game can go as follows:

1. Kf2 Kf7
2. Kg3 Kg7
3. Kh4 Kf7
4. Kh5 Kg7
5. Bg6 Kg8
6. Kh6 Kf8
7. Bh5 Kg8
8. Be7 Kh8
9. Bg4 Kg8
10. Be6 Kh8
11. Bf6#

Scenarios With One Or More Pawns

This is a more likely scenario in most endgames. After much of the board has cleared, there are usually a few Pawns lurking around. Let's examine how best you can utilize them.

Pawn Promotion

This is the best-case scenario for a Pawn in the endgame, so you should pursue it if you can do so without compromising your King.

Let's take an example where there is just one Pawn and no other pieces on the board other than the Kings. From the starting point, you can be able to tell if the Pawn will be able to advance to the other end of the chessboard. If the King is in front of the Pawn with at least one intervening square, then it will be able to successfully make the advance. However, if the opponent's King is directly in front of the Pawn, then the promotion attempt won't be successful. Unless they make a fatal error, the enemy King will be able to keep blocking the Pawn until they force a stalemate or other kind of draw.

In the following image, the Pawn will not be able to get promoted because the black King is directly in front of it:

The pieces in the previous image will move until they get to the positions in the following image:

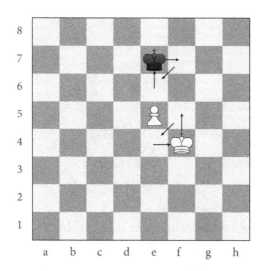

The two Kings will then be stuck repeating the same moves over and over as indicated in the illustration. If the white King tries to move the Pawn two more times, the black King will end up on the eighth rank in front of the Pawn, and that would be a stalemate.

Now, here is an example of a Pawn that might be able to advance to promotion:

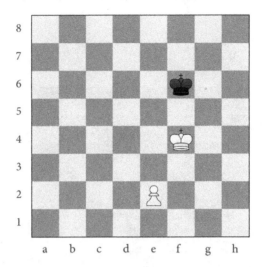

You will notice that the white King is in front of their Pawn, and there is a rank between them to allow for intervention. The white player must be careful to only advance their Pawn when movement is necessary to keep it safe.

As long as the white King stays in front of the Pawn with every move, they can give the Pawn breathing room to come up slowly without falling into the grasp of the black King, and without the black King irreversibly blocking its path. When this play is well executed you may end up with the following scenario:

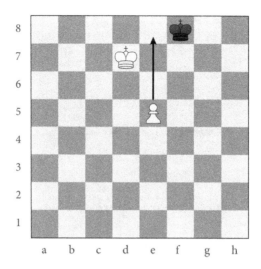

As you can see, the white Pawn has a clear path to promotion, no matter what the black King does.

Let's now look at examples with more than one Pawn on the board:

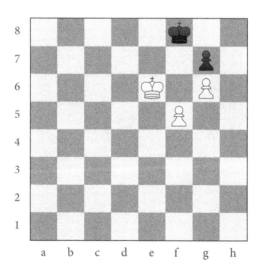

In this case, there are two paths to gaining a Pawn promotion and it requires a lot of skill to figure them out. However, if you understand them and practice them on your board, you will be able to learn how to think several steps ahead.

Here's how the white player can pull off a Pawn promotion in this complex case:

1. Kd7 Kg8
2. Ke7 Kh8
3. f6 Kg8
4. f7 Kh8
5. f7-f8=Q+ ...

In the other option, if the black Pawn captures the white Pawn, the remaining path becomes:

1. f6 gxf6
2. Kf7 f5
3. g7, Kh7
4. g7-g8=Q+ ...

Now that you know how to advance a Pawn to a promotion, consider the following scenario:

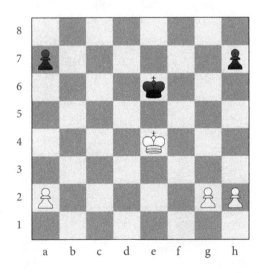

The white player has Pawns on opposite sides of the board. Which one should they advance?

There are some fundamental Pawn principles that you need to know. First, where you are able to advance more than one Pawn, you should prioritize advancing the one without an opposing Pawn. In this case, the Pawn on g2 doesn't have an opposing Pawn on its file, so it's suitable for advancement. Secondly, you should prioritize advancing Pawns on the side of the board where you have superior forces. In this case, the white player has more Pawns on the kingside, so they are better off advancing those Pawns. Therefore on both counts, Pawn g2.

PART 3: GETTING STARTED

Chapter 11: How To Start Playing Chess & Progress To Mastery Level

Since you've come this far, I can confidently inform you that you have adequate theoretical knowledge to start playing chess right now. Congratulations!

You probably have some idea on how you can get started playing the game right now, but in this last chapter, I thought I could offer some suggestions and a little bit of advice on how you can build on your skills.

First, you have to understand that there is a difference between studying chess in theory as we have done in this book, and actually playing the game. Here, we have talked about what moves you should make, and what principles you should apply in different scenarios, but in practice, you are going to be playing against someone (or a computer) that has the same information that you do. So, your edge isn't going to come from theoretical knowledge – your ability to win or lose will depend on how much you practice, and how much thought and calculation you put into each move that you make on the board.

It is for this reason that I recommend you to try practicing on your own for a week or two before you face off with a real-world opponent. If you have a partner or friend that's also getting started, you can let them know about this book so that you both can work through it together, and you can play your first chess matches against each other. If you know someone with advanced chess skills, it is okay to engage them as tutors, but playing against them when you are still figuring things out might only serve to discourage you. Give yourself room to walk before you can fly.

From your very first chess match, you should develop the tendency to strategize instead of relying on instinct or blind luck. Chess is a game of strategy, so your performance should depend on your capacity for strategic thinking, and not your opponent's weaknesses.

When you are confident enough to start playing against people more experienced than you, you'll quickly figure out that there is a psychological element to chess that cannot be adequately covered in a book such as this one. Since you understand chess in theory, you will start to have certain expectations about your opponents' next moves. When dealing with highly skilled players, they can make moves that take you by surprise, or subvert your expectations. You'll also deal with other players that keep you on your toes so that you end up making reactive moves that can throw off your strategy.

To deal with such situations, you need to train yourself to be confident in the moves you make. People have different ways of building confidence, but I personally recommend studying grandmasters. Today, you can find lots of books and online resources with information about how other great chess grandmasters such as Bobby Fischer, Jose' Capablanca, and Garry Kasparov played their games. If you can follow their matches move by move, and comprehend the rationale behind those moves, then you won't be intimidated by regular chess players.

As you start playing chess, you should be prepared to lose. Loss is a part of the game, and the probability of occurrence is pretty high. In fact, if you are not losing most of your chess matches, it means that you are playing against people with a similar or lower skill level as yourself, and you are not challenging yourself as much as you should.

You should also be very particular about the kind of chess that you play as a beginner because that's going to determine how well you do as a learner. There are many variations of chess, and not all of them are good for beginners. You will come across people talking about blitz chess, rapid chess, bullet chess, and regular chess, so let's take a look at each of them.

Blitz chess is also known as speed chess and it refers to a variation of the game whose complexity is compounded by fast time control. Bullet chess is an even speedier variant of blitz chess where each game is limited to just three minutes of play. Games that take less than three minutes are said to have a bullet rating, those that take three to fourteen minutes are said to have a blitz rating, and those that take more than fifteen minutes, but still have time control, are said to have a rapid rating. If you are playing chess online, you are likely to see these ratings or other time pre-sets somewhere on your dashboard. For novice players, these variants of chess are not recommended.

Time controlled chess is really fascinating to watch and fun to play, but it is not meant for beginners. If you have less time to think and make calculations in chess, the quality of your moves is diminished. You are likely to make blunders by failing to consider all possible scenarios in your mind. Even highly experienced players tend to perform worse when they play speed chess. When you are starting out, you need a firm grasp of the principles and fundamentals, and you can't get that if you are racing against the clock.

So, for as long as you consider yourself a beginner, stick to regular chess. Take your time and play out every move in your head before you make it on the board. Getting good at chess is about creating good habits. If you start out by making half thought out moves because you are trying to be fast, the bad habits will stick, and you will have a very difficult time getting rid of them once they have branded themselves in your brain. Right now, even if it takes you a whole minute to figure out your next move, that's okay. After some practice, you will start to notice that you are coming to decisions a lot faster. That means that you are beginning to know the chess principles by heart. Focus on small incremental improvements.

To get adequate and incremental practice, you should consider joining a chess club. There are chess clubs everywhere; in schools, places of work, community centers, parks, and so on. No matter where you are in the world, chances are there are people in your area who meet regularly and play chess. If you are unable to find a physical chess club, you could start one yourself, or find one online.

Once you have some practice under your belt, you should consider entering a chess tournament at the lowest level so see how well you do. Tournaments tend to be set up with certain additional rules that you don't have to stick to when playing casually. For example, they tend to have strict time rules. Competitive chess will help you take your skills to the next level by putting you in a crucible and forcing you to think fast. This will also teach you to keep track of your chess scores so that you can monitor your progress.

If you are unable to join a chess club or find friends to play against, computer chess is always an option. In fact, for a beginner, it may be preferable. With programs such as Microsoft's Chess Titans, you can set them at beginner level and play chess against the computer. You can slowly increase the difficulty level and turn off the hints as you get better at the game. You even have the option of playing chess on your smartphone anywhere and anytime.

Of the many options at your disposal today when it comes to playing chess online, two of the best and most popular ones are the Chess.com app and the Lichess app. On both of these platforms, you will meet an unlimited number of like-minded chess enthusiasts from around the world, who you can play against anytime, night or day. When joining these platforms, make sure to create an account and give an accurate description of your skill level so that you are matched against opponents who are more or less at your level.

Besides one-on-one games, these platforms also have forums and chats where you can ask questions and discuss chess strategies with people who are more experienced in the game.

With all these versatile options at your disposal, you have no reason not to practice. Even with a packed schedule, you can squeeze in a virtual game of chess every day, and you can play one-on-one chess with friends in the evenings or weekends. Mastering chess, just like any other skill, requires deliberate practice, and time dedication. There are a few people who are natural chess prodigies, but the vast majority of the greatest chess players gained their skills through practice. So can you.

Definition Of Terms

The following is a list of chess terms that you'll encounter regularly. Terms that are explained in the book are excluded from this list.

Attack: a move or series of moves that are executed with the intention to threaten or to capture the other player's piece.

Connected Pawns: When at least two Pawns of the same color are on adjacent columns (files), they are said to be connected. They have the ability to offer each other support, which makes them slightly more powerful than Pawns that are isolated.

Development: When a piece is developed, it means it has been put in a position where it's able to have a more active role going forward.

Initiative: A player takes initiative by being proactive and forcing the opponent to be reactive.

Major Pieces: Queens and Rooks.

Minor Pieces: Bishops and Knights.

Piece: The word "piece" is technically used to refer to all pieces in the game except for a Pawn. However, most people don't generally adhere to this strict definition, and they say "piece" in reference to every figurine.

Material: All pieces on the board, especially after considering their relative values. If someone says a player has higher "material value," it means they have a high number of powerful pieces compared to their opponent.

Opposition: When the black and white King are within two squares of each other, they are said to be in opposition. They can't get any closer without going into Check.

Passed Pawn: A Pawn that doesn't have an opposing Pawn on its path, or adjacent to it on the same rank. Such Pawns have a higher likelihood of promotion, which makes them more valuable.

Triangulation: A phenomenon where a piece (most often a King) gets back to the same exact position in 3 moves.

Did you enjoy the book or learn something new? It really helps out small publishers like Grandmaster Chess if you could leave a quick review where you purchased the book so others in the community can also find the book!

CPSIA information can be obtained
at www.ICGtesting.com
Printed in the USA
BVHW040447280321
603587BV00009B/2756